LEARNING HOW TO LEARN

Understanding the secret to learning anything easily

Chloe Gray

DISCLAIMER

This book is written to help you learn anything in life as long as you are willing to learn. However, the level of success you get completely depends on how you put the suggestions written here into **action.**

TABLE OF CONTENT

Introduction: Why should I commit to continuous learning?

As soon as we were born, we begin to learn
But after school, some people quit learning
I have the following question for you
What are YOU currently learning

Your development depends on you actively learning anything in your field or a brand-new hobby

Here are only a few evidence-based advantages of learning:

- We maintain our mental sharpness: Developing new skills increases the amount of myelin (the white matter in our brains that governs mental agility and power).
- We produce better work: Studies reveal that those with more education have more employment options.
- We are happier: According to a different study, education can improve our mental health by giving us a sense of purpose.

One of the quickest methods to increase confidence is to learn.

Learning is one of the finest methods to fight imposter syndrome if you ever experience it.

Before I discovered how to speed up learning, I used to put off learning.

This book offers the top 15 suggestions for quickly learning anything.

TIP 1: The Memory Palace Technique

Consider your house.

You must be able to recall the majority of significant details concerning your home.

The memory palace method comes into play here.

A memory palace is a learning method in which you see a well-known setting and insert mental "things" into it. The memory palace method uses your spatial memory to speed up learning and help you retain new information.

Thanks to Art and Memory, here's how to construct a memory palace.

Step 1: Try selecting a location that you are familiar with for your first memory palace, like your home.

Step 2: Plan out the entire trip. Imagine passing through the front yard, the front door, the living room, and all the other important rooms in your house. Going in a clockwise direction may be advantageous to some people, but it is not required. You will eventually have a lot of memory castles. Don't worry if the memory palace isn't great the first time; you can always update it after testing it a few times.

Step 3: Next, make a list of the information you want to memorize, such as a grocery list with 20 different things such as apples, carrots, bread, milk, and tea.

Step 4: Add a mental representation of each item to each locus in your memory palace, one or two at a time. Exaggerate the depictions of the objects and make them interact with the environment. Imagine several enormous carrots opening up your front door, for instance, if the first item is "carrots" and the front door is the first location in your memory palace.

After you've mastered that, you can link your image to a certain lesson you've learned. For instance, the carrot might need to enter a mathematical calculation into the door lock in order to unlock the front door.

You'll remember what you learn more easily if you do this.

TIP 2: Be a Note Taker

You might be better off writing everything down by hand with paper and a pen if you're used to typing everything you learn.

Because typing doesn't actually teach us very much, that is.

In a 2021 study, typing and handwriting were put to the test:
Students were required to first handwrite notes from a biology textbook after which they are to type them.

The typed notes and the handwritten notes were then put side by side by the researchers.

The outcomes? Researchers discovered that students' typing appeared to be cognitively taxing. In other words, they typed the notes on their computers, but the handwritten notes were more effective when it comes to "retaining" the information.

When typing notes, the students also displayed decreased understanding, terminology correctness, and conceptual flexibility.

Writing everywhere is a pro tip! Write in your journal, on sticky notes, or on a whiteboard, even in the books you are reading.

If you don't read books in print, take a look at the following advice.

TIP 3: Stop being Digital

In relation to handwritten notes, reading real books instead of reading them on a screen may be more beneficial.

In addition to the fact that 90% of college students prefer real books to electronic ones, a psychology lecturer discovered that pupils needed more repetitions when learning from screens than from actual books.

We receive more sensory input from holding and turning pages of books than we would from a digital device, which aids in our ability to remember information.

So, according to science, print books are still useful, especially for improving our learning.

TIP 4: The Interleaving Effect

Are you interested in studying languages?
LingQ estimates that it would take approximately 480 hours to become basic fluent in a language or 720 hours for more challenging languages.

A learning strategy called interleaving involves studying a number of connected subjects at once.

A person learning to swim might include learning the freestyle, breaststroke, and how to float, for instance. An illustration of an interleaving pattern would be as follows:

Learn topic A, then topic B, then topic C, and so on.
Study topic A, then topic B...

Interleaving is effective—possibly better than learning only one subject at a time.

Naturally, researchers put it to the test—in real classrooms. They observed students in one class who took algebra and geometry concurrently and whose weekly homework included a mixture of both types of questions.

The outcome? After a month, they outperformed the standard strategy by 76%.
Interleaving is a fantastic method to liven up the proceedings and improve your learning. Here are a few suggestions you can use:

- Getting into coding? Learn JavaScript, CSS, and HTML as well.
- learning management? Alternate between managerial training, communication skills, and organizational abilities.
- Getting into drawing? Switch between coloring, shadings, and human anatomy.

TIP 5: Take a Break

Do you feel tense? Revved up? Are you in a rush? When you're in that mental state, learning anything is exceedingly difficult.

Stress actively inhibits learning.

Imagine attempting to learn something when agitated, enraged, or trapped in a negative mental pattern.

According to a 2016 study, stress hinders memory retrieval and makes us turn to "rigid, habit-like behavior."

So consider giving your mind a restorative vacation before learning:

- Meditate. Use your preferred meditation method for a brief meditation of five to ten minutes.
- Add some oil. Use essential oils; they smell wonderful.
- Taking a hot bath. Warm baths are excellent for unwinding. Warm baths even lessen tension, anxiety, anger, and melancholy, according to one study, more than a shower alone.

- Take pauses. Try taking a mental break if you are studying for hours on end. Take a stroll outside or implement a time-blocking system for designated breaks.

TIP 6: Test Yourself

Recall those long, restless hours spent studying for a test?

As it happens, testing is effective. According to research, pupils who studied and then took a test had better long-term memory retention than those who did not.

And how should one go about studying for a test?

Learning through an organized, repetitive review of the material to be memorized is known as spaced repetition.

It is beneficial because, unless we evaluate what we have learned, we are likely to forget 20% of what we learn over 24 hours.

After three days, we only recall 60% of what we've learned if we don't test or review it. We will keep the information for longer if we only study it once, but only 60% after seven days.

We can maintain the best level of retention when we plan longer and longer gaps between reviews because we boost memory retention with each additional review. And that's why spaced repetition is so beautiful.

After several reviews, we may eventually only need to go over the subject we learned a few weeks or even months later.

How do you evaluate or test yourself?

TIP 7: Take a Nap

Everyone is aware that a good night's sleep improves performance.

Even a quick nap of 45 to 60 minutes can increase knowledge retrieval from memory five times if you're running on fumes, according to research.

A power nap resets our brain, according to author Daniel Pink's explanation in his book "When: The Scientific Secrets of Perfect Timing." As the day wears on, our brain experiences kink that a power nap can help remove so that we can perform more effectively.

The ideal timeframe for a power nap varies from person to person, but he also suggests a caffeine-nap hack: drink a cup of coffee, then snooze for 25 minutes (the time taken for the caffeine to take effect).

To determine the length of your ideal power nap, try napping.

TIP 8: Own Your Environment

Unbelievably, your surroundings have an impact on how you learn.

Consider yourself in the following environments, for illustration:

- A calm library setting
- Outside, in a park
- In a bustling bistro
- Your own home office desk

Many people operate better in a routine setting that allows them to sit down and concentrate without interruptions. Others might favor a bustling cafe's lively atmosphere.

Your chair is another crucial environmental component because if you work remotely, you'll probably spend most of your days sitting in it.

If you're sitting comfortably, you'll be more inspired to learn instead of complaining about your back.

TIP 9: Explain it Like I'm Five

Robert Feynman, a physicist, developed a method for organization-based learning by making notes on the title page of an empty book.

Feynman was then able to reduce enormously complex concepts to incredibly basic ones.

How?

He employed a strategy I like to refer to as "Explain Like I'm Five." This is how it works:

Consider a challenging concept. Let's use a bonsai tree as our example. Try to simplify the ideas as if you were explaining them to a five-year-old.

Analogies can be used, which is exactly what the Feynman approach is great for. We can say something like: "Bonsai trees are just like a giant tree but smaller" in our situation.

Even though this is oversimplified, breaking out complex ideas into numerous smaller ones might help you see how everything fits together.

Try jotting it down using this method as well if you're having problems visualizing a notion.

TIP 10: The Heart

Do you enjoy working out?

If that's the case, you might learn more effectively.

According to studies, exercise can raise heart rate, which can improve learning capacity.

This is due to the activation of new neurons throughout the learning process.

Additionally, exercise aids in the survival of these brand-new neurons.

So why not work out with your body weight, lift weights, or go for a run in your free time?

If you're studying at your desk, you might want to consider a standing workstation.

You could also use a treadmill to walk on to keep your heart rate high.

TIP 11: Look for your suitable noise

Which learning noise is your favorite?

Some individuals adore listening to music. Some people prefer full silence.

You might be doing it incorrectly if there are construction workers knocking on your front door or if you're used to learning to the sound of noisy '70s hair metal.

While some studies contend that music impairs memory and that people memorize best in silence, others indicate that specific types of music, such as classical music, can enhance memory function.
Who do we then listen to?

Your preferred degree of noise probably depends on your personality type, therefore conduct an experiment to see whether you prefer silence or noise when learning.

TIP 12: Create Learning Stations

Most people like to study in one location, typically at their desks.

However, it could be preferable to alter your surroundings by using what I refer to as "learning stations."

You may set up a study station at your computer desk, another one on the couch, in your favorite neighborhood coffee shop, at the public library, outside on the patio, at your preferred park, etc.

Context-dependent memory is a phenomenon that explains why having numerous learning stations is effective. Our environment and the current knowledge we are learning are connected in our brains, according to research from the University of Wisconsin.

Accordingly, your brain forms more associations with the more diverse contexts you can learn in.

Win-win situation!

TIP 13: Color, lights, Clutter!

Ensure your surroundings are conducive to learning. This includes having the appropriate lighting, colors, and organization:

- Make an effort to learn in a space with natural illumination. According to studies, kids perform 25% better in a setting with natural illumination than they do in a room with dark lighting. For best learning results, study close to windows or in a location with access to sunshine.
- What shade is the setting where you learn? Blue seems to keep us tranquil and at ease. Yellow can uplift and make us feel pleased while red can keep us feeling impassioned. What hue do you prefer? understand which hues are best for learning.
- Eliminate the mess. According to Carnegie Mellon University research, when there is more clutter in the classroom than when it is cleared, students are more easily distracted, spend more time off-task, and learn less. Declutter your environment to free up some of your important mental space.

TIP 14: Learning Stacking

Taking something you already know and picking up new information on related subjects is known as "learning stacking".

For instance, if you're studying cabinet making, you may as well want to learn about the numerous sorts of paints that can be used to color cabinets, the different kinds of trees that are used to make cabinets, the different forms of cabinets that are frequently used around the world, etc.

Building relationship knowledge is a key component of stacking education. Your ability to "connect" new information and better merge it into long-term memory will improve as you increase your knowledge.

I like to compare learning to stack to learning to stack cups subjects, the more substantial the base and the taller your stack will be.

You might want to attempt speed reading to learn even more. The ability to read more quickly by skimming while still taking in what we read is known as speed reading.

TIP 15: Be The guru

If you can pass on what you learn to someone else, fantastic!

If not, research demonstrates that even having the intention to teach someone improves learning capacity.

This is so that we can learn more effectively than, say, someone who only learns to pass tests.

Here are some suggestions for mastering what you're learning:

- Educate a buddy. Do you know someone with whom you can communicate? a relative, close friend, or even your dog? Tell them what you've learned!
- Launch a podcast! A podcast is a simple way to share your knowledge and expand your audience at the same time.
- Create a blog. Use your writing skills to put your understanding into words.

opening a YouTube channel Create a following, participate in the community, and develop into a true authority in your field.

Conclusion: Do We Learn in Different ways?

In essence, some individuals think that people have innate tendencies to learn best through tactile, auditory, or visual encounters.

However, research reveals the opposite: students who chose their preferred learning style and changed their study habits to match it did not significantly improve.

There you have it, then!

I hope this essay was very informative for you and that it motivated you to pursue lifelong learning.

www.ingramcontent.com/pod-product-compliance
Lightning Source LLC
LaVergne TN
LVHW010513160826
845677LV00012B/2827

* 9 7 9 8 3 6 1 6 9 1 5 5 5 *